AFRICA

by Claire Vanden Branden

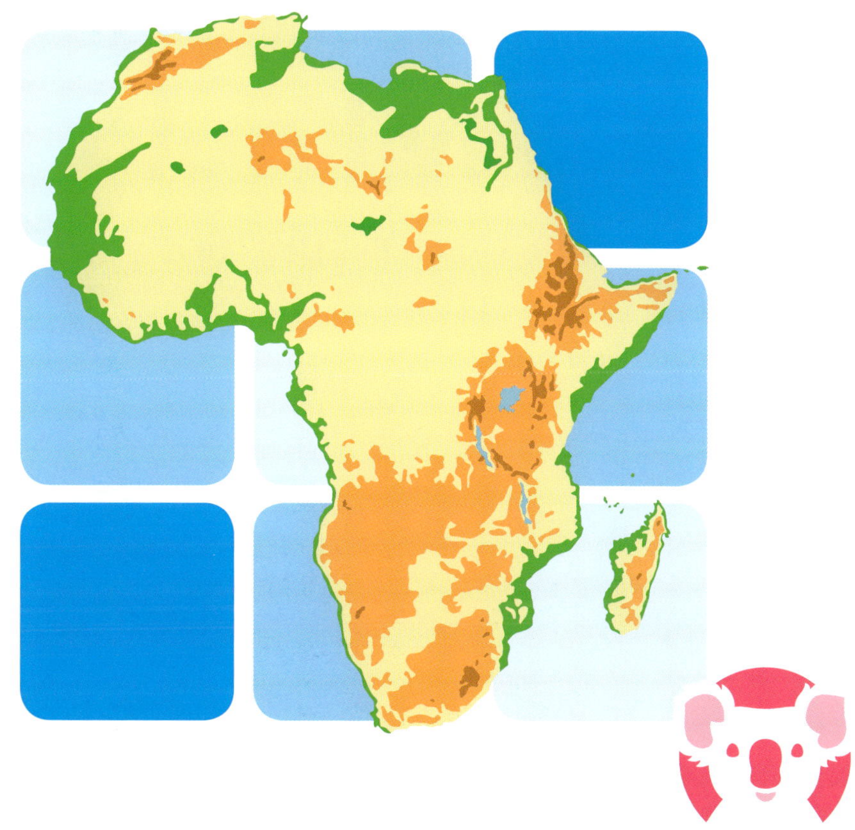

Cody Koala

An Imprint of Pop!
popbooksonline.com

abdobooks.com
Published by Pop!, a division of ABDO, PO Box 398166, Minneapolis, Minnesota 55439.

Printed in the United States of America, North Mankato, Minnesota.

082018
012019

THIS BOOK CONTAINS RECYCLED MATERIALS

Cover Photo: Shutterstock Images
Interior Photos: Shutterstock Images, 1, 5 (top), 5 (bottom right), 9, 13 (top), 13 (bottom left), 13 (bottom right), 14, 18; iStockphoto, 5 (bottom left); Red Line Editorial, 6; Mosa'ab Elshamy/AP Images, 10; Sergio Reboredo/VWPics/AP Images, 17 (top), 17 (bottom left); Artur Widak/Sipa USA/AP Images, 17 (bottom right); Kristin Palitza/picture-alliance/dpa/AP Images, 21

Editor: Charly Haley
Series Designer: Laura Mitchell

Library of Congress Control Number: 2018949236

Publisher's Cataloging-in-Publication Data
Names: Vanden Branden, Claire, author.
Title: Africa / by Claire Vanden Branden.
Description: Minneapolis, Minnesota: Pop!, 2019 | Series: Continents | Includes online resources and index.
Identifiers: ISBN 9781532161698 (lib. bdg.) | 9781641855402 (pbk) | ISBN 9781532162756 (ebook)
Subjects: LCSH: Africa--Juvenile literature. | Continents--Juvenile literature. | Geography--Juvenile literature.
Classification: DDC 916--dc23

Hello! My name is

Cody Koala

Pop open this book and you'll find QR codes like this one, loaded with information, so you can learn even more!

Scan this code* and others like it while you read, or visit the website below to make this book pop.

popbooksonline.com/africa

*Scanning QR codes requires a web-enabled smart device with a QR code reader app and a camera.

Table of Contents

Chapter 1

Africa

Africa is the second-largest **continent** in the world. It has 54 countries. It touches the Atlantic Ocean and the Indian Ocean.

Watch a video here!

MAP OF AFRICA

Africa is next to Europe and Asia. The biggest country in Africa is Algeria. The smallest is Seychelles.

Chapter 2

Hot Savanna

The weather is very hot in Africa. Almost half of Africa is covered in flat grasslands called **savanna**. Much of the other half is **desert**.

savanna in Kenya

Learn more here!

Nile River

The Sahara Desert is the largest desert in Africa. But Africa is not just hot and dry. It has **rain forests** too.

Mount Kilimanjaro is the highest mountain in Africa. Africa also has the world's longest river, the Nile.

Chapter 3

Animals and Plants

Many animals live in Africa. There are elephants, lions, and cheetahs. The dangerous black mamba snake is in Africa.

Cheetahs are fast. They can run as fast as a car driving on a highway.

Learn more here!

The baobab tree is common in Africa. It is called the Tree of Life because it can be used for many things. People eat the tree's fruit and leaves. They can make cloth from the tree's bark.

Chapter 4

People of Africa

More than 1.2 billion people live in Africa. They make up many different groups. Each group has its own history and ways of life.

More than 1,500 languages are spoken in Africa!

Complete an activity here!

In **ancient** times, the people of Egypt built large stone pyramids. The pyramids are still in Africa today.

Botswana is one of the richest countries in Africa. It has a lot of diamonds.

Many people in Africa are very **poor**. Millions of them are **starving**. There are many groups around the world trying to help.

Africa has more people than any other continent except Asia.

Making Connections

Text-to-Self

There are many different animals in Africa. Would you like to see any of them in real life? Which ones would you like to see?

Text-to-Text

Have you read another book about Africa? What did you learn?

Text-to-World

Many people in Africa are poor, but other people are trying to help. Why do you think it's important to help other people in the world?

Glossary

ancient – from a long time ago.

continent – one of the seven large landmasses on Earth.

desert – a very dry area of land where it doesn't rain very often.

poor – having very little money.

rain forest – a tropical forest with many different plants and heavy rainfall.

savanna – a tropical grassland with few trees and little rain.

starving – to suffer from extreme hunger.

Index

Online Resources

popbooksonline.com

Thanks for reading this Cody Koala book!

Scan this code* and others like it in this book, or visit the website below to make this book pop!

*Scanning QR codes requires a web-enabled smart device with a QR code reader app and a camera.